WITHDRAWN

FALLING,

MAY DAY SERMON,

and Other Poems

ALSO BY JAMES DICKEY:

JAMES DICKEY

FALLING,

MAY DAY SERMON,

and Other Poems

 WESLEYAN UNIVERSITY PRESS
Middletown, Connecticut

MANY of these poems first appeared in publications other than volumes by the author. For their courtesy in granting permission to reprint and in assigning copyrights, grateful acknowledgment is made to the editors of the following: *Atlantic Monthly, Beloit Poetry Journal, The Bulletin* (Sydney, Australia), *Choice, Commentary, Encounter, Harper's Magazine, Hudson Review, Kenyon Review, The Nation, The New Yorker, North American Review, Paris Review, Partisan Review, Poetry, Poetry Dial, Quarterly Review of Literature, Saturday Evening Post, Saturday Review, Sewanee Review, Shenandoah, Southern Review, Transatlantic Review, Virginia Quarterly Review,* and *Yale Review.*

Among poems originally printed in *Poetry* are these: "The Being," "A Dog Sleeping on my Feet," "Dover: Believing in Kings," "The Firebombing," "A Folk Singer of the Thirties," "The Hospital Window," "Inside the River," and Part II of "On the Coosawattee."

Poems that first appeared in *The New Yorker* include the following: "Angina," "At Darien Bridge," "The Aura," "A Birth," "Buckdancer's Choice," "Bums, on Waking," "Cherrylog Road," "Coming Back to America," "The Common Grave," "The Driver," "The Dusk of Horses," "Encounter in the Cage Country," "The Escape," "Falling," "False Youth: Two Seasons (II)," "Fence Wire," "For the Nightly Ascent of the Hunter Orion over a Forest Clearing," "Goodbye to Serpents," "The Heaven of Animals," "Hedge Life," "The Ice Skin," "In the Marble Quarry," "In the Mountain Tent," "In the Tree House at Night," "Kudzu," "The Lifeguard," "Listening to Foxhounds," "The Magus," "The Movement of Fish," "The Poisoned Man," "Power and Light," "Reincarnation (I)," "The Salt Marsh," "The Scarred Girl," "The Shark's Parlor," "Snakebite," "Sun," "Them, Crying," "Trees and Cattle," "The Underground Stream," "Walking on Water," "The War Wound," Part I of "On the Coosawattee," and a slightly shorter version of "Slave Quarters."

Library of Congress Cataloging in Publication Data
Dickey, James.
    Falling, may day sermon, and other poems.
      I. Title
PS3554.I32F3   811'.54   81-19861
ISBN 0-8195-5060-4   AACR2
ISBN 0-8195-6069-3 (pbk.)

Manufactured in the United States of America
First edition

To Monroe Spears

Preface

For years, as I read and wrote poetry, a strange kind of object was forming in my mind. Sometimes it was barely present, but at others it seemed almost three-dimensionally real. This was the shape of a solid bank, an on-end block or wall of words, solid or almost solid, black with massed ink, through which a little light from behind would come at intermittent places. Gradually I began to construct such a wall outside myself, at first with words typed and then cut out with scissors and placed in various combinations on a piece of cardboard from a shirt come back from the laundry. The shape of the cardboard was the shape of the poem, and I moved the words around as in a game of metaphysical Scrabble, with the payoff coming in images and new directions of thought from lucky combinations. There was no theme to the first of those poems, but since I had typed and snipped many words that were related to water—or *were* water—the final version had something to do with rain. Though it was not successful enough to publish, I felt that it was promising enough to keep and learn from, which I tried to do. Since cutting out individual words was too laborious and time-consuming, I began to build the walls directly on the page from the typewriter, and spent more and more time erecting them and pushing against them, and trying to peer through them at the place that let the light through. I began to conceive of a poem presented in this way as a confrontation for the reader just as a real wall would be, or one of the paintings of Mark Rothko: a strange and solid obstacle which the reader would not be able to go through, but would have to climb down. Of course one has to "climb down" any page of print—prose or verse—but since I wanted my walls to be rhythmical, to include the recurrent and varied stresses, pauses, onrushes and sound-continuities of a recognizable prosody, the descent would be markedly different from the run-of-the-mill climb-down of a page of prose, or at least I hoped it would. I tried to make it memorable step by step, intending the intermittent light to come strongly and unexpectedly through the places I left blank.

To this concept of the poem-as-barrier, the poetic line is crucial in another sense than it usually is. One of the main virtues of the line is that it increases by a very great deal the memorability of what is being said. I wanted this memorability factor to be powerful, but I thought at first that this might be difficult to assure, since the line went all the way across the page, and was composed of many smaller lines set apart by spaces. But as I continued to work with this form of organization, it seemed to me that in just this fact—the fact that each long page-wide line was comprised of several short "internal" ones—lay the solution to the problem, for the reader could fasten on one fragment within the main line as readily as he could on the whole linear unit, or perhaps even more readily. For example, in the following passage the words, though grouped and spaced irregularly, are presented in their own association within their specific isolated groups and at the same time are contributary to the general structure of the narrative of the girl's fall:

```
. . . for her the ground is closer   water is nearer   she passes
It   then banks   turns   her sleeves fluttering differently as she rolls
Out to face the east, where the sun shall come up from wheatfields   she must
Do something with water   fly to it   fall in it   drink it   rise
From it   but there is none left upon earth   the clouds have drunk it back
The plants have sucked it down . . .
```

Working in this way, I saw that what I wanted was to give each cluster of words its own fierce integrity, and that I was perhaps inadvertently seeking a way to make manifest the characteristics of thought when it associates rapidly, and in detail, in regard to a specific subject, an action, an event, a theme. I envisioned the mind as working by associational and verbal fits and starts, jumps, gaps, and the electric leaps across them: in successive shocks, rests, word-bursts, stamp-printed or lightning-stamped images, crammed clusters. Though I had employed this approach, or something like it, in some of the poems in *Buckdancer's Choice*, I now meant to go the whole way with it, and launched into the two long poems which give this book its title, one the hallucinated version of a girl's fall from an airliner and the other an equally hysterical improvisation on a folk theme from north Georgia, both poems of madness, death, and violent affirmation.

From here, where? I am trying now to work not so much with block-forms and walls of words, but with balance: the balance of the poem on the page which is in some sense analogous to the balance given to the trunk of a tree by its limbs, or by the twigs to the stem. Obviously, all kinds of arrangements of balance can occur, from the obvious to the more irregular and delicate. Around a central bole, sometimes hidden but always present, any number of balancing units can be arranged, and if these are successful in the poems I am writing now and those I plan to write, I hope that the experience of this central stem will be a part of the reader's hidden pleasure: that, and a sense of precariousness, of swaying.

James Dickey
April 1981
Columbia, S.C.

Contents

I Falling

FALLING

*A 29-year-old stewardess fell ... to her
death tonight when she was swept
through an emergency door that sud-
denly sprang open ... The body ...
was found ... three hours after the
accident.*

—*New York Times*

The states when they black out and lie there rolling   when they turn
To something transcontinental   move by   drawing moonlight out
    of the great
One-sided stone hung off the starboard wingtip   some sleeper next to
An engine is groaning for coffee   and there is faintly coming in
Somewhere the vast beast-whistle of space. In the galley with its racks
Of trays   she rummages for a blanket   and moves in her slim tailored
Uniform to pin it over the cry at the top of the door. As though she blew

The door down with a silent blast from her lungs frozen   she is black
Out finding herself   with the plane nowhere and her body taking by
    the throat
The undying cry of the void   falling   living   beginning to be
    something
That no one has ever been and lived through   screaming without
    enough air
Still neat   lipsticked   stockinged   girdled by regulation   her hat
Still on   her arms and legs in no world   and yet spaced also strangely
With utter placid rightness on thin air   taking her time   she holds it
In many places   and now, still thousands of feet from her death
    she seems
To slow   she develops interest   she turns in her maneuverable body

To watch it. She is hung high up in the overwhelming middle of things
    in her
Self   in low body-whistling wrapped intensely   in all her dark
    dance-weight
Coming down from a marvellous leap   with the delaying,
    dumfounding ease
Of a dream of being drawn   like endless moonlight to the harvest soil
Of a central state of one's country   with a great gradual warmth

coming
Over her   floating   finding more and more breath in what she has
      been using
For breath   as the levels become more human   seeing clouds placed
      honestly
Below her left and right   riding slowly toward them   she clasps it all
To her and can hang her hands and feet in it in peculiar ways   and
Her eyes opened wide by wind, can open her mouth as wide   wider
      and suck
All the heat from the cornfields   can go down on her back with a
      feeling
Of stupendous pillows stacked under her   and can turn   turn as
      to someone
In bed   smile, understood in darkness   can go away   slant   slide
Off tumbling   into the emblem of a bird with its wings half-spread
Or whirl madly on herself   in endless gymnastics in the growing
      warmth
Of wheatfields rising toward the harvest moon.   There is time to live
In superhuman health   seeing mortal unreachable lights far down
      seeing
An ultimate highway with one late priceless car probing it   arriving
In a square town   and off her starboard arm the glitter of water catches
The moon by its one shaken side   scaled, roaming silver   My God
      it is good
And evil   lying in one after another of all the positions for love
Making   dancing   sleeping   and now cloud wisps at her no
Raincoat   no matter   all small towns brokenly brighter from inside
Cloud   she walks over them like rain   bursts out to behold a
      Greyhound
Bus shooting light through its sides   it is the signal to go straight
Down like a glorious diver   then feet first   her skirt stripped
      beautifully
Up   her face in fear-scented cloths   her legs deliriously bare   then
Arms out   she slow-rolls over   steadies out   waits for something
      great
To take control of her   trembles near feathers   planes head-down
The quick movements of bird-necks turning her head   gold eyes
      the insight-
eyesight of owls blazing into the hencoops   a taste for chicken
      overwhelming

Her   the long-range vision of hawks enlarging all human lights
     of cars
Freight trains   looped bridges   enlarging the moon racing slowly
Through all the curves of a river   all the darks of the midwest blazing
From above. A rabbit in a bush turns white   the smothering chickens
Huddle   for over them there is still time for something to live
With the streaming half-idea of a long stoop   a hurtling   a fall
That is controlled   that plummets as it wills   turns gravity
Into a new condition, showing its other side like a moon   shining
New Powers   there is still time to live on a breath made of nothing
But the whole night   time for her to remember to arrange her skirt
Like a diagram of a bat   tightly it guides her   she has this flying-skin
Made of garments   and there are also those sky-divers on TV   sailing
In sunlight   smiling under their goggles   swapping batons back
     and forth
And He who jumped without a chute and was handed one by a diving
Buddy. She looks for her grinning companion   white teeth   nowhere
She is screaming   singing hymns   her thin human wings spread out
From her neat shoulders   the air beast-crooning to her   warbling
And she can no longer behold the huge partial form of the world   now
She is watching her country lose its evoked master shape   watching
     it lose
And gain   get back its houses and peoples   watching it bring up
Its local lights   single homes   lamps on barn roofs   if she fell
Into water she might live   like a diver   cleaving   perfect   plunge

Into another   heavy silver   unbreathable   slowing   saving
Element: there is water   there is time to perfect all the fine
Points of diving   feet together   toes pointed   hands shaped right
To insert her into water like a needle   to come out healthily dripping
And be handed a Coca-Cola   there they are   there are the waters
Of life   the moon packed and coiled in a reservoir   so let me begin
To plane across the night air of Kansas   opening my eyes
     superhumanly
Bright   to the dammed moon   opening the natural wings of my jacket
By Don Loper   moving like a hunting owl toward the glitter of water
One cannot just fall   just tumble screaming all that time   one must use
It   she is now through with all   through all   clouds   damp   hair
Straightened   the last wisp of fog pulled apart on her face like wool
     revealing

New darks   new progressions of headlights along dirt roads
   from chaos

And night   a gradual warming   a new-made, inevitable world of
   one's own
Country   a great stone of light in its waiting waters   hold   hold out
For water: who knows when what correct young woman must take up
   her body
And fly   and head for the moon-crazed inner eye of midwest
   imprisoned
Water   stored up for her for years   the arms of her jacket slipping
Air up her sleeves to go   all over her? What final things can be said
Of one who starts out sheerly in her body in the high middle of night
Air   to track down water like a rabbit where it lies like life itself
Off to the right in Kansas? She goes toward   the blazing-bare lake
Her skirts neat   her hands and face warmed more and more by the air
Rising from pastures of beans   and under her   under chenille
   bedspreads
The farm girls are feeling the goddess in them struggle and rise
   brooding
On the scratch-shining posts of the bed   dreaming of female signs
Of the moon   male blood like iron   of what is really said by the moan
Of airliners passing over them at dead of midwest midnight   passing
Over brush fires   burning out in silence on little hills   and will wake
To see the woman they should be   struggling on the rooftree to become
Stars: for her the ground is closer   water is nearer   she passes
It   then banks   turns   her sleeves fluttering differently as she rolls
Out to face the east, where the sun shall come up from wheatfields
   she must
Do something with water   fly to it   fall in it   drink it   rise
From it   but there is none left upon earth   the clouds have drunk
   it back
The plants have sucked it down   there are standing toward her only
The common fields of death   she comes back from flying to falling
Returns to a powerful cry   the silent scream with which she blew down
The coupled door of the airliner   nearly   nearly losing hold
Of what she has done   remembers   remembers the shape at the heart
Of cloud   fashionably swirling   remembers she still has time to die
Beyond explanation. Let her now take off her hat in summer air the
   contour

Of cornfields   and have enough time to kick off her one remaining
Shoe with the toes   of the other foot   to unhook her stockings
With calm fingers, noting how fatally easy it is to undress in midair
Near death   when the body will assume without effort any position
Except the one that will sustain it   enable it to rise   live
Not die   nine farms hover close   widen   eight of them separate,
      leaving
One in the middle   then the fields of that farm do the same   there
      is no
Way to back off   from her chosen ground   but she sheds the jacket
With its silver sad impotent wings   sheds the bat's guiding tailpiece
Of her skirt   the lightning-charged clinging of her blouse   the
      intimate
Inner flying-garment of her slip in which she rides like the holy ghost
Of a virgin   sheds the long windsocks of her stockings   absurd
Brassiere   then feels the girdle required by regulations squirming
Off her: no longer monobuttocked   she feels the girdle flutter   shake
In her hand   and float   upward   her clothes rising off her
      ascending
Into cloud   and fights away from her head the last sharp dangerous
      shoe
Like a dumb bird   and now will drop in   SOON   now will drop

In like this   the greatest thing that ever came to Kansas   down
      from all
Heights   all levels of American breath   layered in the lungs
      from the frail
Chill of space to the loam where extinction slumbers in corn tassels
      thickly
And breathes like rich farmers counting: will come among them after
Her last superhuman act   the last slow careful passing of her hands
All over her unharmed body   desired by every sleeper in his dream:
Boys finding for the first time their loins filled with heart's blood
Widowed farmers whose hands float under light covers to find
      themselves
Arisen at sunrise   the splendid position of blood unearthly drawn
Toward clouds   all feel something   pass over them as she passes
Her palms over *her* long legs   *her* small breasts   and deeply between
Her thighs   her hair shot loose from all pins   streaming in the wind
Of her body   let her come openly   trying at the last second to land

On her back   This is it   THIS
                                    All those who find her impressed
In the soft loam   gone down   driven well into the image of her body
The furrows for miles flowing in upon her where she lies very deep
In her mortal outline   in the earth as it is in cloud   can tell nothing
But that she is there   inexplicable   unquestionable   and remember
That something broke in them as well   and began to live and die more
When they walked for no reason into their fields to where the whole
    earth
Caught her   interrupted her maiden flight   told her how to lie
    she cannot
Turn   go away   cannot move   cannot slide off it and assume another
Position   no sky-diver with any grin could save her   hold her in
    his arms
Plummet with her   unfold above her his wedding silks   she can no
    longer
Mark the rain with whirling women that take the place of a dead wife
Or the goddess in Norwegian farm girls   or all the back-breaking
    whores
Of Wichita. All the known air above her is not giving up quite one
Breath   it is all gone   and yet not dead   not anywhere else
Quite   lying still in the field on her back   sensing the smells
Of incessant growth try to lift her   a little sight left in the corner
Of one eye   fading   seeing something wave   lies believing
That she could have made it   at the best part of her brief goddess
State   to water   gone in headfirst   come out smiling   invulnerable
Girl in a bathing-suit ad   but she is lying like a sunbather at the last
Of moonlight   half-buried in her impact on the earth   not far
From a railroad trestle   a water tank   she could see if she could
Raise her head from her modest hole   with her clothes beginning
To come down all over Kansas   into bushes   on the dewy sixth green
Of a golf course   one shoe   her girdle coming down fantastically
On a clothesline, where it belongs   her blouse on a lightning rod:

Lies in the fields   in *this* field   on her broken back as though on
A cloud she cannot drop through   while farmers sleepwalk without
Their women from houses   a walk like falling toward the far waters
Of life   in moonlight   toward the dreamed eternal meaning of
    their farms
Toward the flowering of the harvest in their hands   that tragic cost

Feels herself go   go toward   go outward   breathes at last fully
Not   and tries   less   once   tries   tries   AH, GOD—

II The Sheep Child and Other Poems

THE SHEEP CHILD

Farm boys wild to couple
With anything   with soft-wooded trees
With mounds of earth   mounds
Of pinestraw   will keep themselves off
Animals by legends of their own:
In the hay-tunnel dark
And dung of barns, they will
Say   I have heard tell

That in a museum in Atlanta
Way back in a corner somewhere
There's this thing that's only half
Sheep   like a woolly baby
Pickled in alcohol   because
Those things can't live. his eyes
Are open   but you can't stand to look
I heard from somebody who . . .

But this is now almost all
Gone. The boys have taken
Their own true wives in the city,
The sheep are safe in the west hill
Pasture   but we who were born there
Still are not sure. Are we,
Because we remember, remembered
In the terrible dust of museums?

Merely with his eyes, the sheep-child may

Be saying   saying

  I am here, in my father's house.
  I who am half of your world, came deeply
  To my mother in the long grass

Of the west pasture, where she stood like moonlight
Listening for foxes. It was something like love
From another world that seized her
From behind, and she gave, not lifting her head
Out of dew, without ever looking, her best
Self to that great need. Turned loose, she dipped her face
Farther into the chill of the earth, and in a sound
Of sobbing   of something stumbling
Away, began, as she must do,
To carry me. I woke, dying,

In the summer sun of the hillside, with my eyes
Far more than human. I saw for a blazing moment
The great grassy world from both sides,
Man and beast in the round of their need,
And the hill wind stirred in my wool,
My hoof and my hand clasped each other,
I ate my one meal
Of milk, and died
Staring. From dark grass I came straight

To my father's house, whose dust
Whirls up in the halls for no reason
When no one comes   piling deep in a hellish mild corner,
And, through my immortal waters,
I meet the sun's grains eye
To eye, and they fail at my closet of glass.
Dead, I am most surely living
In the minds of farm boys: I am he who drives
Them like wolves from the hound bitch and calf
And from the chaste ewe in the wind.
They go into woods   into bean fields   they go
Deep into their known right hands. Dreaming of me,
They groan   they wait   they suffer
Themselves, they marry, they raise their kind.

REINCARNATION (II)

—the white thing was so white, its
wings
so wide, and in those for ever exiled
waters
                              —MELVILLE

As apparitional as sails that cross
Some page of figures to be filed
away
                              —HART CRANE

One can do   one begins to   one can only

Circle   eyes wide with fearing the spirit

Of weight   as though to be born   to awaken to what one is
Were to be carried   passed out
With enormous cushions of air under the arms
Straight up   the head growing stranger
And released between wings near an iceberg

It is too much to ask   to ask
For   under the white mild sun
On that huge frozen point to move

As one is so easily doing

Boring into it with one's new
born excessive eye   after a long
Half-sleeping self-doubting voyage   until
The unbased mountain falters
Turns over like a whale   one screams for the first time

With a wordless voice   swings over
The berg's last treasured bubble
Straightens   wings trembling   RIDING!

Rises into a new South

Sensitive current   checks each wing
It is living there
                                and starts out.

There is then this night
Crawling slowly in under one wing
This night of all nights
Aloft   a night five thousand feet up
Where he soars among the as-yet-unnamed
The billion unmentionable stars
Each in its right relation
To his course   he shivers   changes his heading
Slightly   feels the heavenly bodies
Shake   alter   line up in the right conjunction
For mating   for the plunge
Toward the egg   he soars   borne toward his offspring

By the Dragon balanced exactly
Again the Lion   the sense of the galaxies
Right from moment to moment
Drawing slowly for him a Great
Circle   all the stars in the sky
Embued with the miracle of
The single human Christmas one
Conjoining to stand now over
A rocky island ten thousand
Miles of water away.
                                With a cold new heart
With celestial feathered crutches
A "new start" like a Freudian dream
Of a new start   he hurtles as if motionless
All the air in the upper world
Splitting apart on his lips.

Sleep   *wingless* —NO!
The stars appear, rimmed with red
Space under his breastbone maintains
Itself   he sighs like a man

Between his cambered wings
Letting down now   curving around
Into the wind   slowly toward
Any wave   that—
That one.   He folds his wings and moves
With the mid-Pacific
Carried for miles in no particular direction
On a single wave   a wandering hill
Surging softly along in a powerful
Long-lost phosphorous seethe   folded in those wings
Those ultimate wings   home is like   home is
A folding of wings   Mother
Something whispers   one eye opens   a star shifts
Does not fall   from the eye of the Swan   he dreams

He sees the Southern Cross
Painfully over the horizon   drawing itself
Together   inching
Higher each night of the world   thorn
Points   tilted   he watches   not to be taken in
By the False Cross   as in   in
Another life   not taken

Knowing the true south rises
In a better make of cross   smaller   compact
And where its lights must appear.
Just after midnight he rises
And goes for it   joy with him
Springing out of the water
Disguised as wind   he checks each feather
As the stars burn out   waiting
Taking his course on faith until
The east begins
To pulse with unstoppable light.
Now darkness and dawn melt exactly
Together on one indifferent rill
Which sinks and is
Another   he lives

In renewed light, utterly alone!

In five days there is one ship
Dragging its small chewed off-white
Of ship-water   one candle in a too-human cabin
One vessel moving embedded
In its blue endurable country

Water warms   thereafter it is not
That the sea begins to tinge
Like a vast, laid smoke
But that he closes his eyes and feels himself
Turning whiter and whiter   upheld

At his whitest it is

Midnight   the equator   the center of the world
He sneaks across   afire
With himself   the stars change all their figures
Reach toward him   closer
And now begin to flow
Into his cracked-open mouth   down his throat
A string of lights   emblems   patterns of fire   all
Directions   myths   Hydras
Centaurs   Wolves   Virgins
Eating them all   eating
The void   possessing
Music   order   repose
Hovering   moving on his armbones   crawling
On warm air   covering the whole ocean   the sea deadens
He dulls   new constellations pale off
Him   unmapped roads open out of his breast
Beyond the sick feeling
Of those whose arms drag at treasures   it is like

Roosting   like holding one's arms out
In a clean nightshirt   a good dream   it is all
Instinct   he thinks   I have been born
This way.
                    Goes on
His small head holding
It all   the continents firmly fixed

By his gaze   five new ships turned
Rusty by his rich shadow.
His seamless shoulders of dawn-gold
Open   he opens
Them wider   an inch wider and he would

Trees   voices   white garments   meadows
Fail   under him again are
Mullet believing their freedom
Is to go anywhere they like in their collected shape
The form of an unthrown net
With no net anywhere near them.
Of these he eats.
                    Taking off again
He rocks forward three more days
Twenty-four hours a day
Balancing without thinking—
In doubt, he opens his bill
And vastness adjusts him
He trims his shoulders and planes   up

Up   stalls

In midocean   falls off
Comes down in a long, unbeheld
Curve that draws him deep into

                              evening

Incredible pasture.

The Cross is up.   Looking in through its four panes
He sees something   a clean desk-top
Papers shuffled   hears
Something   a bird word
A too-human word   a word
That should have been somewhere spoken
That now can be frankly said
With long stiff lips into
The center of the Southern Cross
A word enabling one to fly

Out the window of office buildings
Lifts up on wings of its own
To say itself over and over   sails on
Under the unowned stars   sails as if walking
Out the window
That is what I said
That is what I should   that is

Dawn.   Panic   one moment of thinking
Himself in the hell of thumbs   once more   a man
Disguised in these wings   alone   No   again
He thinks   I am here   I have been born
This way   raised up from   raised up in
Myself   my soul
Undivided at last   thrown slowly forward
Toward an unmanned island.

Day overcomes   night comes over
Day with day already

Coming behind it   the sun halved in the east
The moon pressing feathers together.
Who thinks his bones are light
Enough, should try it   it is for everyone
He thinks   the world is for everything born—
I always had
These wings   buried deep in my back:
There is a wing-growing motion
Half-alive in every creature.

Comes down   skims for fifty miles
All afternoon lies skimming
His white shadow burning his breast
The flying-fish darting before him
In and out of the ash-film glaze

Or "because it is there"   into almighty cloud

In rain crying hoarsely
No place to go except

Forward into water in the eyes
Tons of water falling on the back
For hours   no sight   no insight
Beating up   trying
To rise above it   not knowing which way
Is up   no stars   crying
Home   fire   windows   for God
Sake   beating down   up   up-down
No help   streaming   another
Death   vertigo   falling
Upward   mother   God   country
Then seizing one grain of water in his mouth
Glides forward   heavy with cloud
Enveloped   gigantic   blazing with St. Elmo's
Fire   alone at the heart
Of rain   pure bird   heaving up   going

Up from that
                    and from that

Finally breaking

Out   where the sun is violently shining

On the useless enormous ploughland
Of cloud   then up
From just above it   up
Reducing the clouds more and more
To the color of their own defeat
The beauty of history   forgotten bird-
kingdoms packed in batting
The soft country   the endless fields
Raining away beneath him   to be dead
In one life is to enter
Another   to break out   to rise above   the clouds
Fail   pull back their rain

Dissolve.   All the basic blue beneath
Comes back, tattering through. He cries out
As at sight of home   a last human face

In a mirror dazzles   he reaches
Glides off on one wing   stretching himself wider
Floats into night   dark follows
At his pace
                    the stars' threads all connect
On him   and, each in its place, the islands
Rise   small form of beaches

Treeless   tons of guano   eggshells
Of generations
                    down
                              circling

Mistrusting

The land   coming in
Wings ultra-sensitive
To solids   the ground not reflecting his breast
Feet tentatively out
Creaking   close   closer
Earth blurring   tilt back and brace
Against the wind   closest   touch

Sprawl.   In ridiculous wings, he flounders,
He waddles   he goes to sleep
In a stillness of body not otherwhere to be found
Upheld for one night
With his wings closed   the stiff land failing to rock him.

Here mating   the new life
Shall not be lost   wings tangle
Over the beaches   over the pale
Sketches of coral reefs   treading the air
The father moving almost
At once out the vast blue door
He feels it swing open
The island fall off him   the sun

Rise in the shape of an egg   enormous
Over the islands

                    passing out
Over the cliffs   scudding
Fifteen feet from the poor skinned sod
Dazing with purity the eyes of turtles
Lizards   then feeling the world at once
Sheerly restore the sea   the island not
Glanced back at.   where the egg
Fills with almighty feathers
The dead rise, wrapped in their wings
The last thread of white
Is drawn from the foot of the cliffs
As the great sea takes itself back
From around the island

And he sails out   heads north
His eyes already on icebergs
Ten thousand miles off   already feeling
The shiver of the equator as it crosses
His body at its absolute
Midnight whiteness
                         and death also
Stands waiting   years away
In midair   beats
Balanced on starpoints
Latitude and longitude correct
Oriented by instinct   by stars
By the sun in one eye the moon
In the other   bird-death

Hovers for years on its wings
With a time sense that cannot fail
Waits to change
Him again   circles   abides   no feather
Falling   conceived by stars and the void
Is born perpetually
In midair   where it shall be
Where it is.

SUN

O Lord, it was all night
Consuming me   skin crawling tighter than any
Skin of my teeth. Bleary with ointments, dazzling
Through the dark house   man red as iron   glowing
Blazing up anew with each bad
Breath from the bellowing curtains

I had held the sun longer
Than it could stay   and in the dark it turned
My face on, infra-red: there were cracks circling
My eyes where I had squinted
Up from stone-blind sand, and seen
Eternal fire   coronas   huge

Vertical banners of flame
Leap scrollingly from the sun and tatter
To nothing in blue-veined space
On the smoked-crimson glass of my lids.
When the sun fell, I slit my eyeskins
In the dazed ruddy muddle of twilight

And in the mirror saw whiteness
Run from my eyes like tears   going upward
And sideways   slanting   as well as falling,
All in straight lines like rays
Shining   and behind me, careful not
To touch without giving me a chance

To brace myself   a smeared
Suffering woman came merging her flame-shaken
Body halo with mine   her nose still clownish
With oxides: walked to me sweating
Blood, and turned around. I peeled off
Her bathing suit like her skin   her colors

Wincing   she silently biting
Her tongue off   her back crisscrossed with stripes
Where winter had caught her and whipped her.
We stumbled together, and in the double heat
The last of my blond hair blazed up,
Burned off me forever   as we dived

For the cool of the bed
In agony even at holding hands   the blisters
On our shoulders shifting   crackling
Releasing boiling water on the sheets. *O Lord*
Who can turn out the sun, turn out that neighbor's
One bulb on his badminton court

For we are dying
Of light   searing each other   not able
To stop   to get away   she screaming O Lord
Apollo or *Water, Water*   as the moonlight drove
Us down on the tangled grid
Where in the end we lay

Suffering equally   in the sun
Backlashed from the moon's brutal stone
And meeting itself where we had stored it up
All afternoon in pain   in the gentlest touch
As we lay, O Lord,
In Hell, in love.

POWER AND LIGHT

. . . only connect . . .
          —E. M. FORSTER

I may even be
A man, I tell my wife: all day I climb myself
Bowlegged up those damned poles   rooster-heeled in all
Kinds of weather   and what is there when I get
Home? Yes, woman trailing ground-oil
Like a snail, home is where I climb down,
And this is the house I pass through on my way

To power and light.
Going into the basement is slow, but the built-on smell of home
Beneath home gets better with age   the ground fermenting
And spilling through the barrel-cracks of plaster   the dark
Lying on the floor, ready for use   as I crack
The seal on the bottle   like I tell you it takes
A man to pour whiskey in the dark   and CLOSE THE DOOR between

The children and me.
The heads of nails drift deeper through their boards
And disappear. Years in the family dark have made me good
At this   nothing else is so good   pure fires of the Self
Rise crooning in lively blackness   and the silence around them,
Like the silence inside a mouth, squirms with colors,
The marvellous worms of the eye float out into the real

World   sunspots
Dancing as though existence were
One huge closed eye   and I feel the wires running
Like the life-force along the limed rafters   and all connections
With poles   with the tarred naked belly-buckled black
Trees I hook to my heels   with the shrill phone calls leaping
Long distance   long distances through my hands   all connections

Even the one
With my wife, turn good   turn better than good   turn good
Not quite, but in the deep sway of underground   among the roots

That bend like branches   all things connect   and stream
Toward light and speech   tingle   rock like a powerline in wind,
Like a man working, drunk on pine-moves   the sun in the socket
Of his shoulder   and on his neck dancing like dice-dots,

And I laugh
Like my own fate watching over me night and day   at home
Underground   or flung up on towers walking
Over mountains   my charged hair standing on end   crossing
The sickled, slaughtered alleys of timber
Where the lines loop and crackle on their gallows.
Far under the grass of my grave, I drink like a man

The night before
Resurrection Day. My watch glows with the time to rise
And shine. Never think I don't know my profession
Will lift me: why, all over hell the lights burn in your eyes,
People are calling each other   weeping with a hundred thousand
Volts   making deals   pleading   laughing like fate,
Far off, invulnerable   or with the right word pierced

To the heart
By wires I held, shooting off their ghostly mouths,
In my gloves. The house spins   I strap crampons to my shoes
To climb the basement stairs, sinking my heels in the tree-
life of the boards. Thorns! Thorns! I am bursting
Into the kitchen, into the sad way-station
Of my home, holding a double handful of wires

Spitting like sparklers
On the Fourth of July. Woman, I know the secret of sitting
In light   of eating a limp piece of bread   under
The red-veined eyeball of a bulb. It is all in how you are
Grounded. To bread I can see, I say, as it disappears and agrees
With me   the dark is drunk   and I am a man
Who turns on. I am a man.

THE FLASH

Something far off   buried deep and free
In the country   can always strike you dead
Center of the brain. There is never anything

It could be   but you go dazzled
Dazzled   and all the air in that
Direction swarms   waits

For that day-lightning,
For hoe blade   buckle   bifocal
To reach you. Whatever it does

Again is worth waiting for
Worth stopping the car   worth standing alone
For   and arranging the body

For light to score off you
In its own way, and send
Across the wheat   the broad silent

Blue valley, your long-awaited,
Blinding, blood-brotherly
Beyond-speech answer.

ADULTERY

We have all been in rooms
We cannot die in, and they are odd places, and sad.
Often Indians are standing eagle-armed on hills

In the sunrise   open wide to the Great Spirit
Or gliding in canoes   or cattle are browsing on the walls
Far away   gazing down with the eyes of our children

Not far away   or there are men driving
The last railspike, which has turned
Gold in their hands. Gigantic forepleasure lives

Among such scenes, and we are alone with it
At last. There is always some weeping
Between us   and someone is always checking

A wrist watch by the bed to see how much
Longer we have left. Nothing can come
Of this   nothing can come

Of us: of me with my grim techniques
Or you who have sealed your womb
With a ring of convulsive rubber:

Although we come together,
Nothing will come of us. But we would not give
It up, for death is beaten

By praying Indians   by distant cows   historical
Hammers   by hazardous meetings that bridge
A continent. One could never die here

Never die   never die
While crying. My lover, my dear one
I will see you next week

When I'm in town. I will call you
If I can. Please get hold of   please don't
Oh God, Please don't any more I can't bear . . . Listen:

We have done it again   we are
Still living. Sit up and smile,
God bless you. Guilt is magical.

HEDGE LIFE

At morning we all look out
As our dwelling lightens; we have been somewhere.
With dew our porous home
Is dense, wound up like a spring,

Which is solid as motherlode
At night. Those who live in these apartments
Exist for the feeling of growth
As thick as it can get, but filled with

Concealment. When lightning
Strikes us, we are safe; there is nothing to strike, no bole
For all-fire's shattered right arm.
We are small creatures, surviving

On the one breath that grows
In our lungs in the complex green, reassured in the dawn-
silver heavy as wool. We wait
With crowded excitement

For our house to spring
Slowly out of night-wet to the sun; beneath us,
The moon hacked to pieces on the ground.
None but we are curled

Here, rising another inch,
Knowing that what held us solid in the moon is still
With us, where the outside flowers flash
In bits, creatures travel

Beyond us like rain,
The great sun floats in a fringed bag, all stones quiver
With the wind that moves us.
We trade laughters silently

Back and forth, and feel,
As we dreamed we did last night, our noses safe in our fur,
That what is happening to us in our dwelling
Is true: That on either side

As we sleep, as we wake, as we rise
Like springs, the house is winding away across the fields,
Stopped only momentarily by roads,
King-walking hill after hill.

SNAKEBITE

I am the one

And there is no way not
To be me   not to have been flagged

Down from underneath where back
Drop ten deadly and
Dead pine logs   here and where
They have fallen. Now come

To surprise:

Surprise at the dosage   at the shot
In the foot   at the ground

Where I walk   at what
It can do and the ways
Of giving: at dry fish scales
That can float away

In a long dusty arm

Now getting itself   frankly lost
Swimming against the current

Of pinestraw   winging under a stump
And a stone. Here is where
I am the one chosen:
Something has licked my heel

Like a surgeon

And I have a problem with
My right foot and my life.

It is hard to think of dying
But not of killing: hold the good
Foot ready to put on his head
Except that it leaves me only

On a stage of pine logs

Something like an actor   so
Let me sit down and draw

My tiny sword   unfold it
Where the dead sharpen needles
By the million. It is the role
I have been cast in;

It calls for blood.

Act it out before the wind
Blows: unspilt blood

Will kill you. Open
The new-footed tingling. Cut.
Cut deep, as a brother would.
Cut to save it. Me.

BREAD

Old boys, the cracked boards spread before
You, bread and spam   fruit cocktail   powder
Of eggs. I who had not risen, but just come down
From the night sky   knew always this was nothing
Like home   for under the table I was cut deep
    In the shoes

To make them like sandals no stateside store
Ever sold   and my shirtsleeves were ragged as
Though chopped off by propellers in the dark.
It was all our squadron, old boys: it was thus
I sat with you on your first morning
    On the earth,

Old boys newly risen from a B-25 sinking slowly
Into the swamps of Ceram. Patrick said
We got out   we got out on the wings
And lived there   we spread our weight
Thin as we could   arms and legs spread, we lay
    Down night and day,

We lived on the wings. When one of us got to one
Knee to spear a frog   to catch a snake
To eat, we lost another inch. O that water,
He said. O that water. Old boys, when you first
Rose, I sat with you in the mess-tent
    On solid ground,

At the unsinkable feast, and looked at the bread
Given to lizard-eaters. They set it down
And it glowed from under   your tongues
Fluttered   you reached   the scales fell
From your eyes   all of us weightless from living
    On wings so long

No one could escape   no one could sink or swim
Or fly. I looked at your yellow eyeballs
Come up   evolved   drawn out of the world's slime

Amphibious eyes   and Patrick said Bread
Is good   I sat with you in my own last war
     Poem   I closed my eyes

I ate the food I ne'er had eat.

SUSTAINMENT

Here at the level of leaves supposedly for good
Stopped dead on the ground,
From the safety of picturesque height she was suddenly
Falling into the creek, the path
That held her become a flight of dirt. She
And the horse screamed all together, and went down.

Not knowing her, but knowing who she was
Before the creek bank gave
Way and the hooves broke through into creek-shaped air,
I come walking past all the remaining leaves
At the edge, knowing the snow of dirt
Down the bank has long since stopped,

Seeing the gap in the ledge above the stream
Still hold the print
Of a horse's head-down side, aware that I can stoop
With my love, who is with me, and feel
The earth of that blurred impression
Where it is cold with time and many unmeaningful rains.

Love, this wood can support our passion, though leaves
Are not enough death
To balance what we must act out. Let me double down
My autumn raincoat near the summer pit
Where the unknowable woman was riding proudly
The high crest of June, her pink shirt open-throated,

Her four hooves knocking deeply on the earth, the water
Unconsciously holding
Its flow in the pressure of sunlight, a snail
Glinting like a molar at the brink,
And felt it all give way in one clear scream
Lifted out the horse through her lipsticked mouth,

And then, ripping the path clean out of the woods,
Landslid down fifty feet,
Snapping high-grade leather, past any help in the world

As the horse turned over her, in a long changed shape
Loomed once, crossed the sun and the upper trees
Like a myth with a hold on her feet, and fell on her

With all his intended mass. Know, love, that we
Shall rise from here
Where she did not, lying now where we have come
Beneath the scrambling animal weight
Of lust, but that we may sense also
What it involves to change in one half-breath

From a thing half-beast—that huge-striding joy
Between the thighs—
To the wholly human in time
To die, here at this height
Near the vague body-print of a being that struggled
Up, all animal, leaving the human clothes

In their sodden bundle, and wandered the lane of water
Upstream and home,
His bridle dragging, his saddle
Maniacally wrenched, stopping often to drink
Entirely, his eyes receiving bright pebbles,
His head in his own image where it flowed.

A LETTER

Looking out of the dark of the town
At midnight, looking down
Into water under the lighthouse:
Abstractedly, timelessly looking
For something beneath the jetty,
Waiting for the dazed, silent flash,

Like the painless explosion that kills one,
To come from above and slide over
And empty the surface for miles—
The useless, imperial sweep
Of utter light—you see
A thicket of little fish

Below the squared stone of your window,
Catching, as it passes,
The blue afterthought of the blaze.
Shone almost into full being,
Inlaid in frail gold in their floor,
Their collected vision sways

Like dust among them;
You can see the essential spark
Of sight, of intuition,
Travel from eye to eye.
The next leg of light that comes round
Shows nothing where they have been,

But words light up in the head
To take their deep place in the darkness,
Arcing quickly from image to image
Like mica catching the sun:
The words of a love letter,
Of a letter to a long-dead father,

To an unborn son, to a woman
Long another man's wife, to her children,
To anyone out of reach, not born,

Or dead, who lives again,
Is born, is young, is the same:
Anyone who can wait no longer

Beneath the huge blackness of time
Which lies concealing, concealing
What must gleam forth in the end,
Glimpsed, unchanging, and gone
When memory stands without sleep
And gets its strange spark from the world.

THE HEAD-AIM

Sick of your arms,
You must follow an endless track

Into the world that crawls,
That gets up on four legs
When the moon rises from a bed of grass,
The night one vast and vivid
Tangle of scents.

You must throw your arms
Like broken sticks into the alder creek

And learn to aim the head.
There is nothing you can pick up
With fingers any more, nothing
But the new head choked with long teeth,
The jaws, on fire with rabies,

Lifting out of the weeds.
This is the whole secret of being

Inhuman: to aim the head as you should,
And to hold back in the body
What the mouth might otherwise speak:
Immortal poems—those matters of life and death—
When the lips curl back

And the eyes prepare to sink
Also, in the jerking fur of the other.

Fox, marten, weasel,
No one can give you hands.
Let the eyes see death say it all
Straight into your oncoming face, the head
Not fail, not tell.

DARK ONES

We in all lights are coming
Home   transfixed and carried away
From where we work:
                          when the sun moves down
The railroad tracks, and dies a little way
Off in the weeds, lights we have made come on
And carry us: this is how
We are coming, O all
Our dark ones, our darlings.

Now we float down from aircraft

From trains   now at our car
Lights the doors
                  of our home
Garage spring open   we enter and fall
Down in our souls to pray for light
To fail: fail pleasantly with gin,
With problems of children   but fail   fade
Back into our tinted walls:

Let the airports carry it all night

Let the highways support it on their poles
Shining on beer cans
                          rolling drunk in the weeds
After their one fearful bounce:
Lord, let those lights give up
On us: office lights, cast like shade
On fire, from their banks of blue sticks:
A light like the mange, on papers,

On the heads emerging from scratch pads,

Those crammed, volcanic faces
Dreadful to see.
                  All those are creatures
Of light. Let them leave me   let all

Human switches be finally snapped
Off at once   let me go with my dark
Darling, into myself: O let there be
Someone in it with me:

Let us move everything

Off us, and lie touching
With all we have.
                              O creature
Of darkness, let us lie stretched out
Without shadow or weight.
Fasten your hand where my heart
Would burst, if I moved
From your side. You are

Who holds. Hold then   hold my heart

Down from bursting
Into light: hold it still and at rest
In the center of walls
That cannot get their colors
Back without light: O Glory, there is nothing
Yet at the sill   no grain or thread
Of sun   no light as the heart

Beats, feeding from your hand.

ENCOUNTER IN THE CAGE COUNTRY

What I was would not work
For them all, for I had not caught
The lion's eye. I was walking down

The cellblock in green glasses   and came
At last to the place where someone was hiding
His spots in his black hide.

Unchangeably they were there,
Driven in as by eyes
Like mine, his darkness ablaze

In the stinking sun of the beast house.
Among the crowd, he found me
Out   and dropped his bloody snack

And came to the perilous edge
Of the cage, where the great bars tremble
Like wire. All Sunday ambling stopped,

The curved cells tightened around
Us all   as we saw he was watching only
Me. I knew the stage was set, and I began

To perform   first saunt'ring   then stalking
Back and forth like a sentry   faked
As if to run   and at one brilliant move

I made as though drawing a gun from my hip-
bone, the bite-sized children broke
Up   changing their concept of laughter,

But none of this changed his eyes, or changed
My green glasses. Alert, attentive,
He waited for what I could give him:

My moves   my throat   my wildest love,
The eyes behind my eyes. Instead, I left
Him, though he followed me right to the end

Of concrete. I wiped my face, and lifted off
My glasses. Light blasted the world of shade
Back under every park bush   the crowd

Quailed from me   I was inside and out
Of myself   and something was given a life-
mission to say to me hungrily over

And over and over   *your moves are exactly right*
For a few things in this world: we know you
When you come, Green Eyes, Green Eyes.

FOR THE LAST WOLVERINE

They will soon be down

To one, but he still will be
For a little while   still will be stopping

The flakes in the air with a look,
Surrounding himself with the silence
Of whitening snarls. Let him eat
The last red meal of the condemned

To extinction, tearing the guts

From an elk. Yet that is not enough
For me. I would have him eat

The heart, and, from it, have an idea
Stream into his gnawing head
That he no longer has a thing
To lose, and so can walk

Out into the open, in the full

Pale of the sub-Arctic sun
Where a single spruce tree is dying

Higher and higher. Let him climb it
With all his meanness and strength.
Lord, we have come to the end
Of this kind of vision of heaven,

As the sky breaks open

Its fans around him and shimmers
And into its northern gates he rises

Snarling   complete   in the joy of a weasel
With an elk's horned heart in his stomach
Looking straight into the eternal

Blue, where he hauls his kind. I would have it all

My way: at the top of that tree I place

The New World's last eagle
Hunched in mangy feathers   giving

Up on the theory of flight.
Dear God of the wildness of poetry, let them mate
To the death in the rotten branches,
Let the tree sway and burst into flame

And mingle them, crackling with feathers,

In crownfire. Let something come
Of it   something gigantic   legendary

Rise beyond reason over hills
Of ice   SCREAMING   that it cannot die,
That it has come back, this time
On wings, and will spare no earthly thing:

That it will hover, made purely of northern

Lights, at dusk   and fall
On men building roads: will perch

On the moose's horn like a falcon
Riding into battle   into holy war against
Screaming railroad crews: will pull
Whole traplines like fibres from the snow

In the long-jawed night of fur trappers.

But, small, filthy, unwinged,
You will soon be crouching

Alone, with maybe some dim racial notion
Of being the last, but none of how much
Your unnoticed going will mean:

How much the timid poem needs

The mindless explosion of your rage,

The glutton's internal fire   the elk's
Heart in the belly, sprouting wings,

The pact of the "blind swallowing
Thing," with himself, to eat
The world, and not to be driven off it
Until it is gone, even if it takes

Forever. I take you as you are

And make of you what I will,
Skunk-bear, carcajou, bloodthirsty

Non-survivor.
                    Lord, let me die   but not die
Out.

THE BEE

To the football coaches of Clemson College, 1942

One dot
Grainily shifting   we at roadside and
The smallest wings coming   along the rail fence out
Of the woods   one dot   of all that green. It now
Becomes flesh-crawling   then the quite still
Of stinging. I must live faster for my terrified
Small son   it is on him. Has come. Clings.

Old wingback, come
To life. If your knee action is high
Enough, the fat may fall in time   God damn
You, Dickey, *dig*   this is your last time to cut
And run   but you must give it everything you have
Left, for screaming near your screaming child is the sheer
Murder of California traffic: some bee hangs driving

Your child
Blindly onto the highway. Get there however
Is still possible. Long live what I badly did
At Clemson   and all of my clumsiest drives
For the ball   all of my trying to turn
The corner downfield   and my spindling explosions
Through the five-hole over tackle. O backfield

Coach Shag Norton,
Tell me as you never yet have told me
To get the lead out   scream whatever will get
The slow-motion of middle age off me   I cannot
Make it this way   I will have to leave
My feet   they are gone   I have him where
He lives   and down we go singing with screams into

The dirt,
Son-screams of fathers   screams of dead coaches turning
To approval   and from between us the bee rises screaming

With flight   grainily shifting   riding the rail fence
Back into the woods   traffic blasting past us
Unchanged, nothing heard through the air-
conditioning glass   we lying at roadside full

Of the forearm prints
Of roadrocks   strawberries on our elbows as from
Scrimmage with the varsity   now we can get
Up   stand   turn away from the highway   look straight
Into trees. See, there is nothing coming out   no
Smallest wing   no shift of a flight-grain   nothing
Nothing. Let us go in, son, and listen

For some tobacco-
mumbling voice in the branches   to say "That's
a little better,"   to our lives still hanging
By a hair. There is nothing to stop us   we can go
Deep   deeper   into elms, and listen to traffic die
Roaring, like a football crowd from which we have
Vanished. Dead coaches live in the air, son   live

In the ear
Like fathers, and *urge*   and *urge*. They want you better
Than you are. When needed, they rise and curse you   they scream
When something must be saved. Here, under this tree,
We can sit down. You can sleep, and I can try
To give back what I have earned by keeping us
Alive, and safe from bees: the smile of some kind

Of savior—
Of touchdowns, of fumbles, battles,
Lives. Let me sit here with you, son
As on the bench, while the first string takes back
Over, far away   and say with my silentest tongue, with the man-
creating bruises of my arms   with a live leaf a quick
Dead hand on my shoulder, "Coach Norton, I am your boy."

MARY SHEFFIELD

Forever at war news   I am
thinking there   nearly naked
low green of water   hard overflowed forms

water sits running   quietly carving
red rocks forcing white from the current

parts of midstream   join
I sit with one hand   joining
the other hand shyly   fine sand under

still feet   and Mary Sheffield
singing   passed-through

sustained in the   poured forms of live oaks
taking root   in the last tracks
of left and right foot   river flowing

into my mind   nearly naked
the last day but one   before world war.

When the slight wind dies
each leaf still has   two places
such music   touched alive

guitar strings   sounds   join
In the stone's shoal   of swimming

the best twigs I have   the best
sailing leaves   in memory
pass   threading through

all things spread sail   sounds gather
on blunt stone   streaming white

E minor   gently running
I sit with one hand   in the strange life
of the other   watching water throng

on one stone   loving Mary Sheffield
for her chord changes   river always

before war   I sit down and
anywhere   water flows   the breastplate of time
rusts off me   sounds   green forms   low voice

new music   long   long
past.

DEER AMONG CATTLE

Here and there in the searing beam
Of my hand going through the night meadow
They all are grazing

With pins of human light in their eyes.
A wild one also is eating
The human grass,

Slender, graceful, domesticated
By darkness, among the bred-
for-slaughter,

Having bounded their paralyzed fence
And inclined his branched forehead onto
Their green frosted table,

The only live thing in this flashlight
Who can leave whenever he wishes,
Turn grass into forest,

Foreclose inhuman brightness from his eyes
But stands here still, unperturbed,
In their wide-open country,

The sparks from my hand in his pupils
Unmatched anywhere among cattle,

Grazing with them the night of the hammer
As one of their own who shall rise.

THE LEAP

The only thing I have of Jane MacNaughton
Is one instant of a dancing-class dance.
She was the fastest runner in the seventh grade,
My scrapbook says, even when boys were beginning
To be as big as the girls,
But I do not have her running in my mind,
Though Frances Lane is there, Agnes Fraser,
Fat Betty Lou Black in the boys-against-girls
Relays we ran at recess: she must have run

Like the other girls, with her skirts tucked up
So they would be like bloomers,
But I cannot tell; that part of her is gone.
What I do have is when she came,
With the hem of her skirt where it should be
For a young lady, into the annual dance
Of the dancing class we all hated, and with a light
Grave leap, jumped up and touched the end
Of one of the paper-ring decorations

To see if she could reach it. She could,
And reached me now as well, hanging in my mind
From a brown chain of brittle paper, thin
And muscular, wide-mouthed, eager to prove
Whatever it proves when you leap
In a new dress, a new womanhood, among the boys
Whom you easily left in the dust
Of the passionless playground. If I said I saw
In the paper where Jane MacNaughton Hill,

Mother of four, leapt to her death from a window
Of a downtown hotel, and that her body crushed-in
The top of a parked taxi, and that I held
Without trembling a picture of her lying cradled
In that papery steel as though lying in the grass,
One shoe idly off, arms folded across her breast,
I would not believe myself. I would say
The convenient thing, that it was a bad dream

Of maturity, to see that eternal process

Most obsessively wrong with the world
Come out of her light, earth-spurning feet
Grown heavy: would say that in the dusty heels
Of the playground some boy who did not depend
On speed of foot, caught and betrayed her.
Jane, stay where you are in my first mind:
It was odd in that school, at that dance.
I and the other slow-footed yokels sat in corners
Cutting rings out of drawing paper

Before you leapt in your new dress
And touched the end of something I began,
Above the couples struggling on the floor,
New men and women clutching at each other
And prancing foolishly as bears: hold on
To that ring I made for you, Jane—
My feet are nailed to the ground
By dust I swallowed thirty years ago—
While I examine my hands.

COMING BACK TO AMERICA

We descended the first night from Europe   riding the ship's sling
Into the basement.   Forty floors of home weighed on us.   We broke
    through
To a room, and fell to drinking madly with all those boozing, reading
The Gideon Bible in a dazzle of homecoming scripture   Assyrian
    armies
The scythes of chariots blazing like the windows of the city   all cast
Into our eyes in all-night squinting barbaric rays of violent unavoidable
    glory.
There were a "million dollars in ice cubes" outside our metal door;
The dead water clattered down hour after hour as we fought with
    salesmen
For the little blocks that would make whole our long savage drinks.
I took a swaying shower, and we packed the whole bathroom of towels
    into
Our dusty luggage, battling paid-for opulence with whatever weapon
Came to hand.   We slept; I woke up early, knowing that I was
    suffering
But why not. My breath would not stir, nor the room's.   I sweated
Ice in the closeness   my head hurt with the Sleep of a Thousand Lights
That the green baize drapes could not darken.   I got up, bearing
Everything   found my sharp Roman shoes   went out   following
    signs
That said Swimming Pool.   Flashing bulbs on a red-eyed panel,
    I passed
Through ceiling after ceiling of sleeping salesmen and whores, and
    came out
On the roof.   The pool water trembled with the few in their rooms
Still making love.   This was air.   A skinny girl lifeguard worked
At her nails; the dawn shone on her right leg in a healthy, twisted flame.
It made me squint   slick and lacquered with scars   with the wild
    smoky city
Around it   the great breath to be drawn above sleepers   the hazy
Morning towers.   We sat and talked   she said a five-car wreck
Of taxis in Bensonhurst had knocked her out and taken her kneecap
But nothing else.   I pondered this   the sun shook off a last heavy
Hotel   and she leapt and was in the fragile green pool as though
I were still sleeping it off eleven floors under her: she turned in a water

Ballet by herself   graceful   unredeemable   her tough face exactly
As beautiful and integral as the sun come out of the city.   Vulnerable,
Hurt in my country's murderous speed, she moved   and I would have
    taken
Her in my arms in water throbbing with the passion of travelling men,
Unkillable, both of us, at forty stories in the morning   and could have
Flown with her   our weightlessness preserved by the magic pool
    drawn from
Under the streets   out of that pond   passing over the meaningless
Guardrail   feeling the whole air pulse like water sleepless with
    desperate
Love-making   lifting us out of sleep into the city summer dawn
Of hundreds of feet of gray space spinning with pigeons now under
Us   among new panels of sun in the buildings blasting light silently
Back and forth across streets between them: could have moved with her
In all this   over the floods of glare raised up in sheets   the gauze
Distances where warehouses strove to become   over the ship I had
    ridden
Home in   riding gently   whitely   beneath.   Ah, lift us, green
City water, as we turn the harbor around with our legs   lazily changing
The plan of the city with motions like thistles   like the majestic swirl
Of soot   the winged seed of pigeons   and so would have held her
As I held my head   a-stammer with light   defending it against the
    terrible
Morning sun of drinkers   in that pain, exhalting in the blind notion
Of cradling her somewhere above ships and buses   in the air like a
    water
Ballet   dancing deep among the dawn buildings in a purely private
Embrace of impossibility   a love that could not have been guessed:
Woman   being   idea   temple dancer   tough girl from Bensonhurst
With a knee rebuilt out of sunlight   returned-to amazement
    O claspable
Symbol   the unforeseen on home ground   The thing that sustains
    us forever
In other places!

THE BIRTHDAY DREAM

At the worst place in the hills above the city
Late at night I was driving   cutting through
The overbalancing slums. There was no soul or body
In the streets. I turned right   then left somewhere
Near the top, dead-ending into a wall. A car
Pulled out and blocked me. Four men detached from it.
I got out too. It was Saturday night   the thrill
Of trouble shimmered on the concrete. One shadow
Had a bottle of wine. I stood and said, say, Buddy,
Give me a drink of that wine   not at all fearing
Shaking   as on anything but dream bones   dream
Feet I would have. He said, We're looking for somebody
To beat up. It won't be me, I said   and took him
By the arm with one hand and tossed him into the air.
Snow fell from the clearness in time for there
To be a snowbank for him to fall into elbow-first.
He got up, holding the wine. This guy is too big,
He said, he is too big for us; get the Professor.
Four of us stood together as the wind blew and the snow
Disappeared   and watched the lights of the city
Shine   some others appearing   among them   some
Going out   and watched the lava-flow of headlights off
In the valley. Like a gunshot in the building next to us
A light went out   and down came a middle-aged man
With a hairy chest; his gold-trimmed track shorts had
YMCA Instructor on them   and I knew it was time
For the arm game. We stretched out on our stomachs
On top of the dead-end wall. On one side was the drop
We had all been looking into   and the other side sank
Away with my car   with the men: two darks lifted
Us toward the moon. We put our elbows on the wall
And clasped palms. Something had placed gold-rimmed
Glasses of wine beside us   apartment lights hung in them
Loosely   and we lay nose to nose at the beginning

Of that ceremony; I saw the distant traffic cross him
From eye to eye. Slowly I started to push   and he
To push. My body grew as it lay   forced against his
But nothing moved. I could feel the blood vessels
In my brow distend   extend   grow over the wall like vines
And in my neck   swell like a trumpet player's: I gritted
Into his impassive face   where the far lights moved   this is
What I want   this is what I came for. The city pulsed
And trembled in my arm   shook with my effort   for miles
In every direction   and from far below in the dark
I heard the voices of men raised up in a cry of wild
Encouragement   of terror   joy   as I strained to push
His locked hand down. I could not move him   did not want
To move him   would not yield. The world strove with my body
To overcome   the highways shuddered   writhed   came apart
At the centerline   far below us a silent train went by
A warning light   and slowly from the embodying air was loaded
With thousands of ghostly new cars   in tiered racks
The light like pale wine in their tinted windshields.
The culture swarmed around me like my blood   transfigured
By force. I put my head down and pushed with all my life
And writing sprang under my forehead   onto the concrete:
Graffitti scratched with a nail   a boot heel   an ice pick
A tire iron   a scrap of metal from a stolen car   saying
You are here   and I woke
Entangled with my wife, who labored   pled   screamed
To bring me forth. The room was full of mildness. I was forty.

FALSE YOUTH: TWO SEASONS

I have had my time   dressed up as something else,
Have thrown time off my track by my disguise.
This can happen when one puts on a hunter's cap,
An unearned cowboy hat   a buckskin coat   or something
From outer space, that a child you have got has got
For Christmas. It is oddest and best in the uniform
Of your country   long laid in boxes and now let out
To hold the self-betrayed form in the intolerant shape
Of its youth.   I have had my time doing such,

Sitting with Phyllis Huntley as though I were my own
Son surrounded by wisteria   hearing mosquitoes without
The irritation middle age puts on their wings: have sat
By a big vine going round the rotten, imperial pillars
Of southern Mississippi. All family sounds drew back

Through the house in time to leave us hanging
By rusty chains. In the dark, dressed up in my militant youth,
I might have just come down from the black sky   alive
With an ancient war   dead with twenty million   twenty
Years ago   when my belt cried aloud for more holes
And I soft-saluted every changing shape   that saluted me,
And many that did not: every tree   pole   every bush
Of wisteria   as I came down from the air toward some girl

Or other. Decked out in something strange my country
Dreamed up   I have had my time in that swing,
The double chair that moves at the edge of dark
Where the years stand just out of range of house-
light, their hands folded at their fat waists, respectful
As figures at a funeral. And from out of the air an enormous
Grin came down, to remake my face   as I thought of children
Of mine almost her age   and a mosquito droned like an immortal
Engine. I have had my time of moving back and forth
With Phyllis Huntley   and of the movement of her small hand
Inside mine, as she told me how she learned to work
An electric computer in less than two afternoons of her job

At the air base. The uniform tightened as I sat
Debating with a family man away from home. I would not listen
To him, for what these boys want is to taste a little life
Before they die: that is when their wings begin to shine
Most brilliantly from their breasts into the darkness
And the beery breath of a fierce boy demands of the fat man
He's dying of   more air   more air   through the tight belt
Of time   more life   more now   than when death was faced
Less slowly   more now than then   more now.

WINTER

Through an ice storm in Nashville I took a student home,
Sliding off the road twice or three times; for this
She asked me in. She was a living-in-the-city
Country girl   who on her glazed porch broke off
An icicle, and bit through its blank bone: brought me
Into another life   in the shining-skinned clapboard house
Surrounded by a world where creatures could not stand,
Where people broke hip after hip. At the door my feet
Took hold, and at the fire I sat down with her blind
Grandmother. All over the double room were things
That would never freeze, but would have taken well
To ice: long tassels hanging from lamps   curtains
Of beads   a shawl on the mantel   all endless things
To touch   untangle   all things intended to be
Inexhaustible to hands. She sat there, fondling
What was in reach   staring into the fire with me
Never batting a lid. I talked to her easily   eagerly
Of my childhood   my mother whistling in her heartsick bed
My father grooming his gamecocks. She rocked, fingering
The lace on the arm of the chair   changing its pattern
Like a game of chess. Before I left, she turned and raised
Her hands, and asked me to bend down. An icicle stiffened
In my stomach   as she drew on my one lock of hair
Feeling the individual rare strands   not pulling any
Out. I closed my eyes as she put her fingertips lightly
On them   and saw, behind sight   something in me   fire
Swirl in a great shape like a fingerprint   like none other
In the history of the earth   looping   holding its wild lines
Of human force. Her forefinger   then her keen nail

Went all the way along the deep middle line of my brow
Not guessing but knowing   quivering   deepening
Whatever I showed by it. She said, you must laugh a lot
Or be in the sun, and I began to laugh quietly against
The truth, so she might feel what the line she followed
Did then. Her hands fell   and she said to herself, My God,
To have a growing boy. You cannot fool the blind, I knew
As I battled for air   standing   laughing a lot as she
Said I must do   squinting also as in the brightest sun
In Georgia   to make good   to make good the line in my head.
She lifted her face like a swimmer; the fire swarmed
On my false, created visage   as she rocked and took up
The tassel of a lamp. Some kind of song may have passed
Between our closed mouths as I headed   into the ice.
My face froze with the vast world of time   in a smile
That has never left me since my thirty-eighth year
When I skated like an out-of-shape bear to my Chevrolet
And spun my wheels on glass: that time when age was caught
In a thaw in a ravelling room   when I conceived of my finger
Print as a shape of fire   and of youth as a lifetime search
For the blind.

III May Day Sermon

MAY DAY SERMON TO THE WOMEN
OF GILMER COUNTY, GEORGIA,
BY A WOMAN PREACHER LEAVING THE BAPTIST CHURCH

Each year at this time I shall be telling you of the Lord
—Fog, gamecock, snake and neighbor—giving men all the help they
    need
To drag their daughters into barns. Children, I shall be showing you
The fox hide stretched on the door   like a flying squirrel   fly
Open   to show you the dark where the one pole of light is paid out
In spring by the loft, and in it the croker sacks sprawling and shuttling
Themselves into place as it comes   comes   through spiders dead
Drunk on their threads   the hogs' fat bristling   the milk
Snake in the rafters unbending through gnats to touch the last place
Alive on the sun with his tongue   I shall be flickering from my mouth
Oil   grease cans   lard cans   nubbins   cobs   night
Coming   floating   each May with night coming I cannot help
Telling you how he hauls her to the centerpole   how the tractor moves
Over as he sets his feet and hauls   hauls   ravels her arms and hair
In stump chains: Telling: telling of Jehovah come and gone
Down on His belly   descending   creek-curving   blowing His legs

Like candles, out   putting North Georgia copper on His head
To crawl in under the door in dust red enough to breathe
The breath of Adam into: Children, be brought where she screams
    and begs
To the sacks of corn and coal   to nails   to the swelling ticks
On the near side of mules, for the Lord's own man has found the limp
Rubber that lies in the gulley   the penis-skin like a serpent
Under the weaving willow.
                      Listen: often a girl in the country,
Mostly sweating   mostly in spring, deep enough in the holy Bible
Belt, will feel her hair rise up   arms rise, and this not any wish

Of hers, and clothes like lint shredding off her   abominations
In the sight of the Lord: will hear the Book speak like a father
Gone mad: each year at this time will hear the utmost sound
Of herself, as her lungs cut, one after one, every long track
Spiders have coaxed from their guts   stunned spiders fall
Into Pandemonium   fall   fall   and begin to dance like a girl

On the red clay floor of Hell   she screaming   her father screaming
Scripture   CHAPter and verse   beating it into her with a weeping
Willow branch   the animals stomping   she prancing and climbing
Her hair   beasts shifting from foot to foot about the stormed
Steel of the anvil   the tractor gaslessly straining   believing
It must pull up a stump   pull   pull down the walls of the barn
Like Dagon's temple   set the Ark of the Lord in its place   change all
Things for good, by pain. Each year at this time you will be looking up
Gnats in the air   they boil   recombine   go mad with striving
To form the face of her lover, as when he lay at Nickajack Creek
With her by his motorcycle   looming   face trembling with exhaust
Fumes   humming insanely—each May you hear her father scream
     like God
And King James as he flails   cuds richen   bulls chew themselves
     whitefaced
Deeper into their feed bags, and he cries something the Lord   cries
Words! Words! Ah, when they leap   when they are let out of the
     Bible's
Black box   they whistle   they grab the nearest girl and do her hair up
For her lover in root-breaking chains   and she knows she was born
     to hang
In the middle of Gilmer County   to dance, on May Day, with holy
Words all around her   with beasts with insects   O children NOW
In five bags of chicken-feed the torsos of prophets form   writhe
Die out as her freckled flesh   as flesh and the Devil twist and turn
Her body to love   cram her mouth with defiance   give her words
To battle with the Bible's in the air: she shrieks sweet Jesus and God
I'm glad   O my God-darling   O lover   O angel-stud   dear heart
Of life put it in me   *give*   you're killing   KILLING: each
Night each year at this time I shall be telling you of the snake-
doctor drifting from the loft, a dragonfly, where she is wringing
Out the tractor's muddy chains   where her cotton socks prance,
Where her shoes as though one ankle were broken, stand with night
Coming   and creatures drawn by the stars, out of their high holes
By moon-hunger driven   part the leaves   crawl out of Grimes Nose
And Brasstown Bald: on this night only I can tell how the weasel pauses
Each year in the middle of the road   looks up at the evening blue
Star   to hear her say again   O again   YOU CAN BEAT ME
     TO DEATH
And I'll still be glad:

Sisters, it is time to show you rust
Smashing the lard cans more in   spring after spring   bullbats
Swifts   barn swallows   mule bits clashing on walls   mist turning
Up white out of warm creeks: all over, fog taking the soul from the body
Of water   gaining   rising up trees   sifting up through smoking green
Frenzied levels of gamecocks sleeping from the roots   stream-curves
Of mist: wherever on God's land is water, roads rise up the shape of
     rivers
Of no return: O sisters, it is time   you cannot sleep with Jehovah

Searching for what to be, on ground that has called Him from His Book:
Shall He be the pain in the willow, or the copperhead's kingly riding
In kudzu, growing with vines toward the cows   or the wild face
     working over
A virgin, swarming like gnats   or the grass of the west field, bending
East, to sweep into bags and turn brown   or shall He rise, white on
     white,
From Nickajack Creek as a road?   The barn creaks like an Ark   beasts
Smell everywhere the streams drawn out by their souls   the flood-
sigh of grass in the spring   they shall be saved   they know as she
     screams
Of sin   as the weasel stares   the hog strains toward the woods
That hold its primeval powers:
                              Often a girl in the country will find
     herself
Dancing with God in a mule's eye, twilight drifting in straws from the
     dark
Overhead of hay   cows working their sprained jaws sideways at the
     hour
Of night all things are called: when gnats in their own midst and fury
Of swarming-time, crowd into the barn   their sixty-year day consumed
In this sunset   die in a great face of light that swarms and screams
Of love.
               Each May you will crouch like a sawhorse to make yourself
More here   you will be cow chips   chickens croaking for her hands
That shook the corn over the ground   bouncing   kicked this way
And that, by the many beaks   and every last one of you will groan
Like nails barely holding   and your hair be full of the gray
Glints of stump chains.   Children, each year at this time you shall have
Back-pain, but also heaven   but also   also this lovely other life-

pain between the thighs: woman-child or woman in bed in Gilmer
County   smiling in sleep like blood-beast and Venus together
Dancing the road as I speak, get up   up in your socks and take
The pain you were born for: that rose through her body straight
Up from the earth like a plant, like the process that raised overhead
The limbs of the uninjured willow.
                                        Children, it is true
That the kudzu advances, its copperheads drunk and tremendous
With hiding, toward the cows   and wild fences cannot hold the string
Beans as they overshoot their fields: that in May the weasel loves love
As much as blood   that in the dusk bottoms young deer stand half
In existence, munching cornshucks   true that when the wind blows
Right   Nickajack releases its mist   the willow-leaves stiffen once
More   altogether   you can hear   each year at this time you can hear
No   Now, no   Now   Yes   Again   More   O   O my God
I love it   love you   don't leave   don't   don't stop O GLORY
Be:
        More dark   more coming   fox-fire crawls over the okra-
patch   as through it a real fox creeps to claim his father's fur
Flying on doornails   the quartermoon on the outhouse begins to shine
With the quartermoonlight of this night   as she falls and rises,
Chained to a sapling like a tractor   WHIPPED for the wind in the
    willow
Tree   WHIPPED for Bathsheba and David   WHIPPED for the
    woman taken
Anywhere   anytime   WHIPPED for the virgin sighing   bleeding
From her body   for the sap and green of the year   for her own good
And evil:
        Sisters, who is your lover? Has he done nothing but come
And go?   Has your father nailed his cast skin to the wall as evidence
Of sin?   Is it flying like a serpent in the darkness   dripping pure
    radiant venom
Of manhood?
                Yes, but *he* is unreeling in hills between his long legs
The concrete of the highway   his face in the moon beginning
To burn   twitch   dance like an overhead swarm   he feels a nail
Beat through his loins far away   he rises in pain and delight, as spirit
Enters his sex   sways   forms   rises with the forced, choked, red
Blood of her red-headed image, in the red-dust, Adam-colored clay
Whirling and leaping   creating   calling: O on the dim, gray man-

track of cement flowing into his mouth   each year he turns the moon
    back
Around on his handlebars   her image going all over him like the wind
Blasting up his sleeves. He turns off the highway, and
                                                            Ah, children,
There is now something élse to hear: there is now this madness of
    engine
Noise in the bushes   past reason   ungodly   squealing   reverting
Like a hog turned loose in the woods   Yes, as he passes the first
Trees of God's land   game-hens overhead   and the farm is ON
Him   everything is more   *more*   MORE as he enters the black
Bible's white swirling ground   O daughters   his heartbeat great
With trees   some blue leaves coming   NOW   and right away fire
In the right eye   Lord   more   MORE   O Glory   land
Of Glory: ground-branches hard to get through   coops where
    fryers huddle
To death, as the star-beast dances and scratches at their home-boards,
His rubber stiffens on its nails: Sisters, understand about men and
    sheaths:

About nakedness: understand how butterflies, amazed, pass out
Of their natal silks   how the tight snake takes a great breath   bursts
Through himself and leaves himself behind   how a man casts finally
Off everything that shields him from another   beholds his loins
Shine with his children forever   burn with the very juice
Of resurrection: such shining is how the spring creek comes
Forth from its sunken rocks   it is how the trout foams and turns on
Himself   heads upstream, breathing mist like water, for the cold
Mountain of his birth   flowing   sliding in and through the ego-
maniacal sleep of gamecocks   shooting past a man with one new blind
Side   who feels his skinned penis rise like a fish through the dark
Woods, in a strange lifted-loving form   a snake about to burst
Through itself on May Day   and leave behind on the ground   still
Still   the shape of a fooled thing's body:
                                              he comes on   comes
Through the laurel, wiped out on his right by an eye-twig   now he
Is crossing the cow track   his hat in his hand going on before
His face   then up   slowly over   over like the Carolina moon
Coming into Georgia   feels the farm close its Bible and ground-
fog over him   his dark side blazing   something whipping

By, beyond sight: each year at this time I shall be letting you
Know when she cannot stand   when the chains fall back on
To the tractor   when you should get up   when neither she nor the
    pole
Has any more sap   and her striped arms and red hair must keep her
From falling   when she feels God's willow laid on her, at last,
With no more pressure than hay, and she has finished crying to her
    lover's
Shifting face   and his hand when he gave it   placed it, unconsumed,
In her young burning bush.   Each year by dark she has learned

That home is to hang in   home is where your father cuts the baby
Fat from your flanks for the Lord, as you scream for the viny foreskin
Of the motorcycle rider. Children, by dark   by now, when he drops
The dying branch and lets her down   when the red clay flats
Of her feet hit the earth   all things have heard—fog, gamecock
Snake and lover—and we listen: Listen, children, for the fog to lift
The form of sluggish creeks into the air: each spring, each creek
On the Lord's land flows in two   O sisters, lovers, flows in two
Places: where it was, and in the low branches of pines where chickens
Sleep in mist   and that is where you will find roads floating free
Of the earth   winding   leading unbrokenly out of the farm of God
The father:
                    Each year at this time she is coming from the barn   she
Falls once, hair hurting her back   stumbles walking naked
With dignity   walks with no help to the house   lies face down
In her room, burning   tuning in   hearing in the spun rust-
groan of bedsprings, his engine root and thunder like a pig,
Knowing who it is   must be   knowing that the face of gnats will wake
In the woods, as a man: there is nothing else this time of night
But her dream of having wheels between her legs: tires, man,
Everything she can hold, pulsing together   her father walking
Reading   intoning   calling   his legs blown out by the ground-
fogging creeks of his land: Listen   listen like females each year
In May   O glory   to the sound   the sound of your man gone wild
With love in the woods   let your nipples rise   and leave your feet
To hear: This is when moths flutter in from the open, and Hell
Fire of the oil lamp shrivels them   and it is said
To her: said like the Lord's voice trying to find a way
Outside the Bible   O sisters   O women and children who will be

Women of Gilmer County   you farm girls and Ellijay cotton mill
Girls, get up   each May Day   up in your socks   it is the father
Sound   going on about God   making, a hundred feet down,
The well beat its bucket like a gong: she goes to the kitchen,
Stands with the inside grain of pinewood whirling on her like a cloud
Of wire   picks up a useful object   two   they are not themselves
Tonight   each hones itself as the moon does   new by phases
Of fog   floating unchanged into the house   coming atom
By atom   sheepswool   different smokes   breathed like the Word
Of nothing, round her seated father. Often a girl in the country,
Mostly in spring   mostly bleeding   deep enough in the holy Bible
Belt   will feel her arms rise up   up   and this not any wish
Of hers   will stand, waiting for word.   O daughters, he is rambling
In Obadiah   the pride of thine heart hath deceived thee, thou
That dwelleth in the clefts of the rock, whose habitation is high
That saith in his heart   O daughters   who shall bring me down
To the ground?   And she comes down   putting her back into
The hatchet   often   often   he is brought down   laid out
Lashing   smoking   sucking wind: Children, each year at this time
A girl will tend to take an ice pick in both hands   a lone pine
Needle   will hover   hover: Children, each year at this time
Things happen quickly   and it is easy for a needle to pass
Through the eye of a man bound for Heaven   she leaves it   naked goes
Without further sin through the house   floating in and out of all
Four rooms   comes onto the porch on cloud-feet   steps down and out
And around to the barn   pain changing   her old screams hanging
By the hair around her: Children, in May, often a girl in the country
Will find herself lifting wood   her arms like hair rising up
To undo locks   raise latches   set gates aside   turn all things
Loose   shoo them out   shove   pull   O hogs are leaping ten
Million years back through fog   cows walking worriedly   passing out
Of the Ark   from stalls where God's voice cursed and mumbled
At milking time   moving   moving   disappearing   drifting
In cloud   cows in the alders already lowing far off   no one
Can find them each year: she comes back to the house and grabs double
Handfuls of clothes
                    and her lover, with his one eye of amazing grace
Of sight, sees her coming as she was born   swirling   developing
Toward him   she hears him grunt   she hears him creaking

His saddle   dead-engined   she conjures one foot whole from the
     ground-
fog to climb him behind   he stands up   stomps   catches   roars
Blasts the leaves from a blinding twig   wheels   they blaze up
Together   she breathing to match him   her hands on his warm belly
His hard blood renewing like a snake   O now   now as he twists
His wrist, and takes off with their bodies:
                              each May you will hear it
Said that the sun came as always   the sun of next day burned
Them off with the mist: that when the river fell back on its bed
Of water   they fell from life   from limbs   they went with it
To Hell   three-eyed   in love, their legs around an engine, her arms
Around him.   But now, except for each year at this time, their sound
Has died: except when the creek-bed thicks its mist   gives up
The white of its flow to the air   comes off   lifts into the pinepoles
Of May Day   comes back as you come awake in your socks and
     crotchhair
On new-mooned nights of spring   I speak   you listen and the pines
     fill
With motorcycle sound as they rise, stoned out of their minds on the
     white
Lightning of fog   singing   the saddlebags full of her clothes
Flying   snagging   shoes hurling away   stockings grabbed-off
Unwinding and furling on twigs: all we know   all we could follow
Them by was her underwear   was stocking after stocking where it tore
Away, and a long slip stretched on a thorn   all these few gave
Out. Children, you know it: that place was where they took
Off into the air   died   disappeared   entered my mouth   your mind
Each year   each pale, curved breath   each year as she holds him
Closer wherever he hurtles   taking her   taking her   she going
     forever
Where he goes   with the highways of rivers   through one-eyed
Twigs   through clouds of chickens   and grass with them bends
Double   the animals lift their heads   peanuts and beans exchange
Shells in joy   joy like the speed of the body and rock-bottom
Joy: joy by which the creek bed appeared to bear them out of the Bible
's farm   through pine-clouds of gamecocks where no earthly track
Is, but those risen out of warm currents   streams born to hang
In the pines of Nickajack Creek: tonight her hands are under
His crackling jacket   the pain in her back enough to go through

Them both   her buttocks blazing in the sheepskin saddle: tell those
Who look for them   who follow by rayon stockings   who look on
    human
Highways   on tracks of cement and gravel   black weeping roads
Of tar: tell them that she and her rider have taken no dirt
Nor any paved road   no path for cattle   no county trunk or trail
Or any track upon earth, but have roared like a hog on May Day
Through pines and willows: that when he met the insane vine
Of the scuppernong   he tilted his handlebars back and took
The road that rises in the cold mountain spring from warm creeks:
O women in your rayon from Lindale, I shall be telling you to go
To Hell   by cloud   down where the chicken walk is running
To weeds   and anyone can show you where the tire marks gave out
And her last stocking was cast   and you stand as still as a weasel
Under Venus   before you dance   dance yourself blue with blood-
joy looking into the limbs   looking up into where they rode
Through cocks tightening roots with their sleep-claws. Children,
They are gone: gone as the owl rises, when God takes the stone
Blind sun off its eyes, and it sees   sees hurtle in the utter dark
Gold of its sight, a boy and a girl buried deep in the cloud
Of their speed   drunk, children   drunk with pain and the throttle
Wide open, in love   with a mindless sound   with her red hair
In the wind streaming gladly for them both   more than gladly
As the barn settles under the weight of its pain   the stalls fill once
More with trampling like Exodus   the snake doctor gone the rats
    beginning
On the last beans   and all the chicks she fed, each year at this time
Burst from their eggs as she passes:
                              Children, it is true that mice
No longer bunch on the rafters, but wade the fields like the moon,
Shifting in patches   ravenous   the horse floats, smoking with flies,
To the water-trough   coming back less often   learning to make
Do with the flowing drink of deer   the mountain standing   cold
Flowing into his mouth   grass underfoot   dew   horse or what
ever he is now   moves back into trees where the bull walks
With a male light spread between his horns   some say screams like
    a girl
And her father yelling together:
                              Ah, this night in the dark laurel
Green of the quartermoon I shall be telling you that the creek's last

Ascension is the same   is made of water and air   heat and cold
This year as before: telling you not to believe every scream you hear
Is the Bible's: it may be you or me   it may be her sinful barn-
howling for the serpent, as her father whips her, using the tried
And true rhythms of the Lord.   Sisters, an old man at times like this
Moon, is always being found   yes found with an ice-pick on his mind,
A willow limb in his hand.   By now, the night-moths have come
Have taken his Bible and read it   have flown, dissolved, having found
Nothing in it for them.   I shall be telling you at each moon   each
Year at this time, Venus rises   the weasel goes mad at the death
In the egg, of the chicks she fed for him by hand: mad in the middle
Of human space he dances   blue-eyed   dances with Venus rising
Like blood-lust over the road   O tell your daughters   tell them
That the creek's ghost can still   O still can carry double
Weight of true lovers   any time   any night as the wild turkeys claw
Into the old pines of gamecocks   and with a cow's tongue, the Bible
    calls
For its own, and is not heard   and even God's unsettled great
    white father-
head with its ear to the ground, cannot hear   know   cannot pick
Up where they are   where her red hair is streaming through the white
Hairs of His centerless breast: with the moon   He cries with the
    cow all
Its life penned up with Noah in the barn   talk of original
Sin as the milk spurts   talk of women   talk of judgment and flood
And the promised land:
                              Telling on May Day, children: telling
That the animals are saved without rain   that they are long gone
From here   gone with the sun   gone with the woman taken
In speed   gone with the one-eyed mechanic   that the barn falls in
Like Jericho at the bull's voice   at the weasel's dance   at the hog's
Primeval squeal   the uncut hay walks when the wind prophesies in
    the west
Pasture   the animals move   roam, with kudzu creating all the
    earth
East of the hayfield: Listen: each year at this time the county speaks
With its beasts and sinners   with its blood: the county speaks of
    nothing
Else each year at this time: speaks as beasts speak to themselves
Of holiness learned in the barn: Listen   O daughters   turn   turn

74

In your sleep   rise with your backs on fire   in spring   in your socks
Into the arms of your lovers: every last one of you, listen one-eyed
With your man   in hiding   in fog where the animals walk through
The white breast of the Lord   muttering   walk with nothing
To do but be   in the spring laurel in the mist and self-sharpened
Moon   walk through the resurrected creeks   through the Lord
At their own pace   the cow shuts its mouth and the Bible is still
Still open at anything   we are gone   the barn wanders over the earth.